BIGGEST NAMES IN SPORTS

BRYCE HARPER
BASEBALL STAR

by Marty Gitlin

FOCUS
READERS

North Star
EDITIONS

WWW.NORTHSTAREDITIONS.COM

Produced for North Star Editions by Red Line Editorial.

Photographs ©: Pablo Martinez Monsivais/AP Images, cover, 1; Alex Brandon/AP Images, 4–5, 6, 16–17, 22–23; Josh Holmberg/Icon Sportswire, 8–9, 11; Seth Poppel/Yearbook Library, 12; Isaac Brekken/AP Images, 15; Tom DiPace/AP Images, 19; David Hood/Cal Sports Media/AP Images, 25; Red Line Editorial, 29

ISBN
978-1-63517-041-2 (hardcover)
978-1-63517-097-9 (paperback)
978-1-63517-199-0 (ebook pdf)
978-1-63517-149-5 (hosted ebook)

Library of Congress Control Number: 2016951013

Printed in the United States of America
Mankato, MN
November, 2016

ABOUT THE AUTHOR
Marty Gitlin is a sportswriter and educational book author based in Cleveland, Ohio. He has had more than 100 books published, including dozens about famous athletes.

TABLE OF CONTENTS

CHAPTER 1

GOING DEEP

Fans of the Washington Nationals know better than to look away when Bryce Harper steps to the plate. They might see something special anytime he bats.

One example happened in September 2015. The Nationals were playing the Atlanta Braves. In the first inning, Harper faced pitcher Julio Teheran.

Bryce Harper watches his home run against the Braves sail out of the ballpark.

Harper is greeted by his Nationals teammates after rounding the bases.

Teheran, a right-hander, fired a fastball. Harper unleashed his picture-perfect left-handed swing.

The ball soared 453 feet (138 m) and landed in the upper deck in right field.

Teheran looked back to watch its flight for just a second. He knew it was long gone. He had just given up the longest home run Harper had ever hit in the big leagues. And that's saying something. Harper is known for a lot of things, but hitting a baseball a long way is probably first on the list.

STAR-SPANGLED BATTER

The Nationals were playing in the nation's capital on July 4, 2015. Harper wanted to do something special for Independence Day. So he used a bat with stars and stripes and the skyline of Washington, DC, painted on the barrel. Then he blasted a home run against San Francisco Giants ace Madison Bumgarner.

CHAPTER 2

SUPERSTAR IN THE MAKING

When he was a boy growing up in Las Vegas, Nevada, it was clear from early on that Bryce Harper was special. At age three he played T-ball against six-year-olds. And he was the best player on the field.

Bryce practiced baseball constantly, most of the time with his father, Ron.

Harper rounds the bases while playing for Las Vegas High School.

They worked on hitting. They worked on throwing. They worked on fielding. Ron drove Bryce to **clinics** and **tournaments**.

Bryce **excelled** in youth baseball events all over the country. In one tournament in Alabama, he came to bat 12 times. Bryce had 12 hits, and 11 of them were home runs.

Las Vegas High School baseball coach Sam Thomas ran four-hour practices. When practice was over, Bryce would race to his dad's truck. They left together for more batting practice.

Thomas knew he had a star in the making. He allowed Bryce to play practice games with his team when Bryce was

Harper was a catcher in his younger days.

only an eighth grader. Bryce **dominated** the older players. He drew attention from major league **scouts** at age 13.

Two coaches measured one blast Harper launched as a freshman. It landed in the desert well past the baseball field.

Harper played for Team USA in the 2008 Youth Pan Am games.

The ball had traveled 570 feet (174 m). Legendary New York Yankees **slugger** Mickey Mantle hit the longest home run in major league history. It was estimated at 565 feet (172 m).

Bryce showed his skills on a bigger stage that summer. Playing for the US under-16 national team, he dominated the 2008 Youth Pan American Championships in Veracruz, Mexico. He batted .571 and hit four home runs in eight games. He stole six bases in six tries. Bryce even pitched for Team USA. He often thanked the fans by signing autographs deep into the night.

Then Bryce came home and posted an amazing batting average of .569 as a sophomore. He worked harder than ever. The rest of the world began to take notice as well. *Sports Illustrated* splashed Bryce's picture on its cover in June 2009.

Bryce played with incredible confidence and fire. He said his goal was to be the greatest baseball player of all time.

Bryce was only a high school sophomore. But he was ready to play at a higher level. So he passed a test to graduate from high school early. He then enrolled at the College of Southern Nevada.

When he joined the Southern Nevada team, Bryce was the age of most high school juniors. It didn't matter. He batted .442 with 29 home runs in just 62 games. He led the team with 18 stolen bases. He proved to be a fine catcher. He threw bullets to second base to nail runners

Harper played one year of college baseball—when he was just 17 years old.

trying to steal. He also proved to be a clutch hitter. Harper slammed four home runs in a regional title game.

It came as no surprise when Bryce was named conference Most Valuable Player (MVP). He even earned a perfect 4.0 grade point average in his first semester of college. He was doing everything well. And he was ready for the next step.

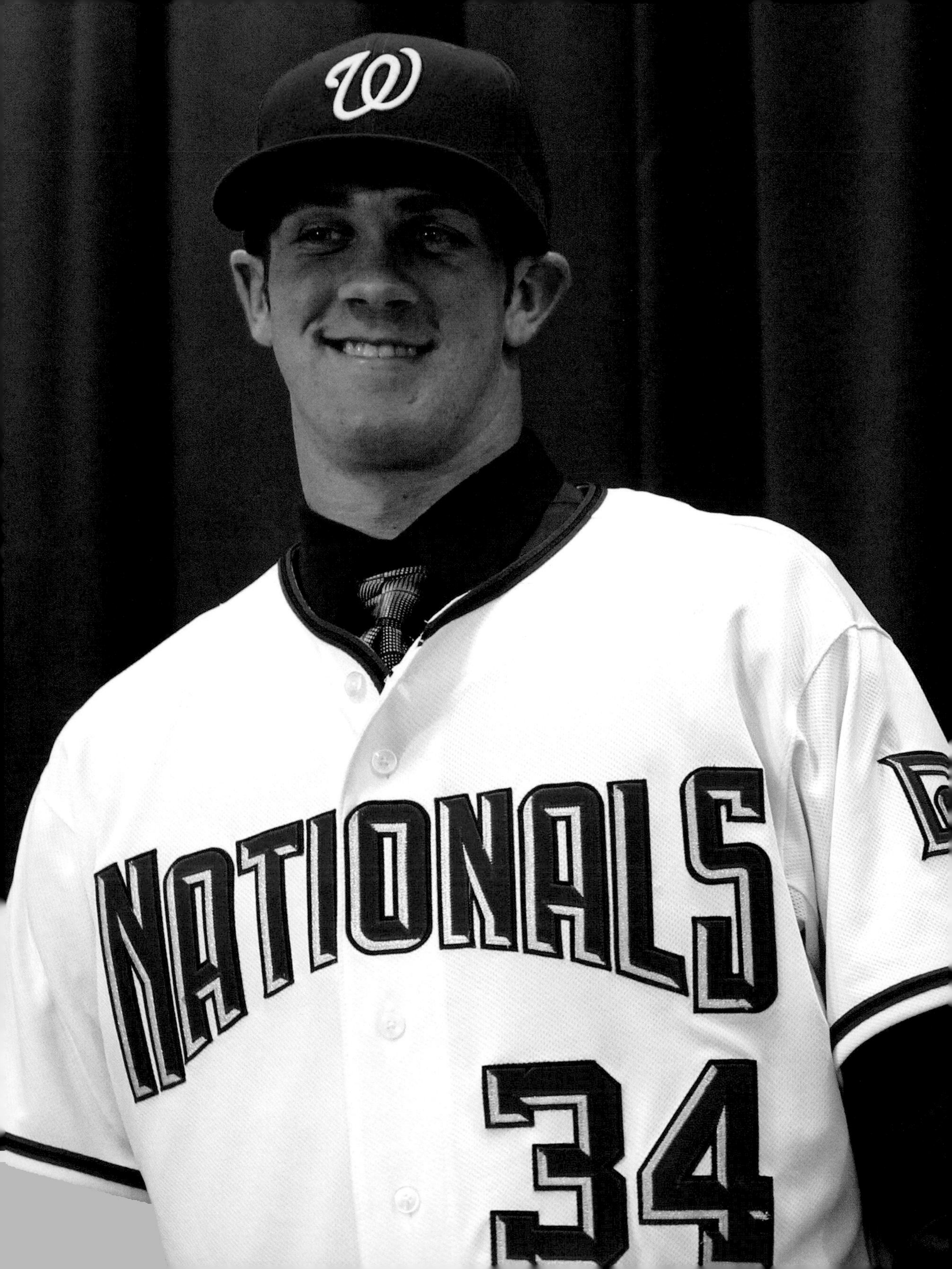
NATIONALS
34

CHAPTER 3

TURNING PRO

Bryce Harper drew big crowds when he played at Southern Nevada. But fans weren't the only ones packing the stands. An average of 10 major league scouts kept tabs on Bryce's talent during every game. And at least 10 teams sent their general manager to watch Bryce play.

Harper models his new Nationals jersey after being chosen with the first pick of the 2010 MLB draft.

They wanted to see for themselves if the stories they'd been hearing were true.

Of course, they liked what they saw. One scout said he had not seen a player that talented in 30 years. So it wasn't much of a surprise when the Washington Nationals took Harper with the first pick in the 2010 Major League Baseball (MLB) **draft**.

But the Nationals did not want Harper to play catcher. That position is hard on the body. The Nationals moved him to the outfield. That would allow him to work on becoming the best hitter he could be. Although he liked catching, Bryce agreed to the switch.

Harper took to his new position in the outfield quickly.

Harper played his first full season in the minor leagues at age 18. He posted a .297 batting average and 17 home runs in 387 at-bats. The Nationals realized that Harper was ready for a bigger challenge.

Early in the 2012 season, they promoted the 19-year-old to the big leagues. He showed he was ready.

Harper made his major league debut against the Los Angeles Dodgers at famed Dodger Stadium. He stepped to the plate in the seventh inning of his first game. He peered out at Dodgers pitcher Chad Billingsley, who threw a fastball. Harper took his usual powerful swing. The ball rocketed off his bat and landed near the fence in center field. Harper ran so hard that his helmet fell off as he pulled into second base with a double.

Major league pitchers are a lot better than minor leaguers, and Harper had his struggles adjusting in his first season. But he provided steady production. He performed well enough to win National League (NL) Rookie of the Year honors. He was already a star. But it would take him a few more years and a few bumps in the road to become a superstar.

GOOD WITH THE GLOVE

Harper is known more for his hitting than for any other part of his game. But he has worked hard to become a good defensive outfielder. His speed helps him track down balls in the gaps, and his strong arm keeps runners from trying to take extra bases. Harper can help his team win even if he's not having a good day at the plate. "My attitude is if I don't get a hit, nobody is getting a hit," he said.

CHAPTER 4

MVP SEASON

Pitchers don't want to throw a hanging curveball to Bryce Harper. In 2013, Miami Marlins pitcher Ricky Nolasco learned that in the first inning of the season's first game.

Nolasco threw Harper a pitch that just hung in the strike zone. Harper blasted it into the right field seats for a home run.

Harper shows off his NL Rookie of the Year Award on Opening Day 2013.

Harper hit another home run in the fourth inning. The Nationals won the game 2–0.

Harper was becoming a baseball hero. But Harper's Heroes was important, too. That was the **charity** organization he started in 2013 to help children battling cancer. His work allows kids to attend a Nationals game. They get a pass to watch batting practice on the field and meet Harper before the game.

Harper played hard and he played well. But he struggled to stay healthy. His **aggressive** style led to numerous injuries. In 2013, he banged his knee twice running into outfield walls while trying to make a catch. His knee bothered

Teammate Denard Span and the Nationals' trainer check on Harper after he crashed into the wall.

him the rest of the year. The next year, Harper injured his thumb sliding into third base. He needed surgery to repair it, and he was sidelined for nine weeks.

But Harper was healthy all through the 2015 season. He heated up in early May and his bat stayed hot the rest of the year.

Harper had a three-homer game against Miami. He hit six home runs in a three-game stretch in May. He had an amazing 22 hits in 39 at-bats in one stretch. He went on another tear in September, hitting 9 homers in 12 games. The crowd loved it. The Nationals drew 2.6 million fans to their 81 home games that year. Harper always made sure to put on a show for them.

After the season, Harper earned the biggest honor a baseball player can receive. He was voted the NL MVP.

Harper followed his MVP season by helping the Nationals win their division for the third time in five years. He also played in his fourth All-Star game.

Harper's teammates marvel at what he does on the field. They also appreciate what he does off the field. Giving back to the community and helping others in need remain his top priorities. Time will tell if he achieves his goal of becoming the greatest baseball player of all time.

HELPING HAND

Harper gets a lot of pleasure helping kids fight cancer. He understands the importance of what he does. "I enjoy making their days, making them smile," he said. "There are a lot of other things in life [besides] baseball."

BRYCE HARPER

- Height: 6 feet 3 inches (191 cm)
- Weight: 215 pounds (98 kg)
- Birth date: October 16, 1992
- Birthplace: Las Vegas, Nevada
- High school: Las Vegas High School
- College: Southern Nevada (2009–10)
- MLB team: Washington Nationals (2012–)
- Major awards: 2012 NL Rookie of the Year;
  2015 NL MVP

Las Vegas

Washington, DC

FOCUS ON
BRYCE HARPER

Write your answers on a separate piece of paper.

1. Write a letter to a friend describing what you learned about Bryce Harper.

2. Do you think the Nationals made the right decision when they moved Bryce Harper from catcher to the outfield? Why or why not?

3. Who did Bryce Harper play against in his first major league game?

      A. Los Angeles Dodgers
      B. Miami Marlins
      C. Atlanta Braves

4. Why did Bryce Harper skip his last two years of high school?

      A. He wasn't a very good student.
      B. He was ready to face better competition.
      C. He didn't like practicing for four hours a day.

Answer key on page 32.